C000268798

INTRODUCTION

The Lord Mayor and Lady Mayoress use the Mansion House as their home during their year of office, and they and their staff work there. Consequently, many of the rooms described in this guide are never shown to visiting members of the public. They have nevertheless been included to give visitors as complete an account as possible of the house and to help them understand the changes which have taken place there over the years.

The Mansion House is open by appointment for visits by organised groups. Applications should be made in writing to
The Principal Assistant
The Mansion House
London EC4N 8BH

Access and facilities for disabled people are available.

Transport

Cannon Street British Rail and Cannon Street and Bank underground stations are close by and there are frequent bus services to Bank.

The 1746 Roque map of the City showing the location of the Mansion House

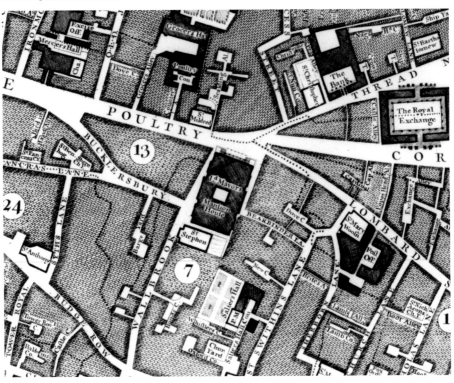

HISTORY AND LOCATION

From the time it was first occupied in 1752, the Mansion House has been one of the grandest Georgian town palaces in London and is recognised today as a building of great national importance. It survives, relatively unchanged, in the heart of the modern City of London and is still in everyday use as the residence of the Lord Mayor, who lives and works there, using the house as a splendid setting for many of the City's ceremonial occasions.

Before the Mansion House was built, each Lord Mayor carried out his mayoral duties from his own private house, using the hall of his Livery Company or Guildhall for larger entertainments and ceremonies. The building of a house for the Lord Mayor was suggested immediately after the Great Fire of London in 1666 and discussions continued for a number of years.

Other cities were considering providing residences for their mayors at this time. In 1715, Dublin purchased a town house for its Mayor, and the City of York began to build a Mansion House in 1725. Doncaster Mansion House was begun in 1745. None of these was as large as the London Mansion House, and none had such grand rooms for entertainments. The City of London's increasing power and influence made it ever more important for its Mayor to be housed in appropriate state.

James Gibbs was asked for designs in 1728 but it was only in 1735 that the project was seriously considered. A committee was appointed by the Court of Common Council

> 'to Consider of a proper Place or Places whereon to Erect a Mansion House ... and to procure a Plan or Plans for such intended Building'.

Work then started in earnest to find a suitable site and design. Of the three possible sites – Gresham College, Leadenhall Market and the Stocks Market – the Mansion House Committee rejected the first almost immediately. Gresham College was inconveniently situated on the edge of the City and was protected under the terms of Sir Thomas Gresham's will. The other two sites received more prolonged consideration. Leadenhall Market was large but was composed of a number of substantial buildings. Replacements would have been needed for these and the resulting site would have been inconveniently and irregularly shaped.

The site finally chosen – that of the Stocks Market – was smaller and was closely surrounded by other buildings but it was of a more regular shape. In addition, most of the land was already in the City's possession, there were few permanent buildings to be taken down and it was centrally placed at the junction of several large thoroughfares, with the new Bank of England building opposite.

ARCHITECTURE

The Lord Mayor's new residence was no ordinary town house. It needed not only living and working accommodation for the Lord Mayor and his household, but also ample room for civic, ceremonial and large entertainments, and a Justice Room where the Lord Mayor could hear cases in his role as Chief Magistrate of the City of London. Above all, it needed to announce the importance of the City to its citizens and the world outside its walls. The chief officers of the Lord Mayor's household, the Swordbearer and the Common Cryer, suggested that accommodation be arranged around a courtyard, with a great hall behind – a form traditional in the City. However,

Portrait of George Dance the Elder by Nathaniel Dance

they made no recorded suggestions as to architectural style.

Designs were submitted by several architects in a variety of styles. In 1737 the City of London eventually chose a design by George Dance the Elder in preference to those submitted by James Gibbs, John James, Isaac Ware, Giacomo Leoni, Batty Langley and Captain de Berlain. Dance was probably favoured because he had recently taken over the post of Clerk of the City's Works, was acquainted with the workings of the City, and produced a design which provided the Mayoralty with the kind of accommodation it needed, in a building with a striking silhouette.

The fashionable style of the time was English Palladianism, derived not only from the works of the famous sixteenth century Italian architect Andrea Palladio, but also from those by Inigo Jones, architect to Charles I. Three of its principal exponents in the early eighteenth century were the Earl of Burlington, Colen Campbell and William Kent, all of whom were still alive when Dance created his design. His plan was probably drawn from that of Palladio's Palazzo Valmarana, his main elevation from Campbell's Wanstead House, Essex, and the side elevations from the south front of Wilton House, Wiltshire, thought to be by Inigo Jones and much quoted by the eighteenth-century Palladians. The interiors were inspired by the designs of

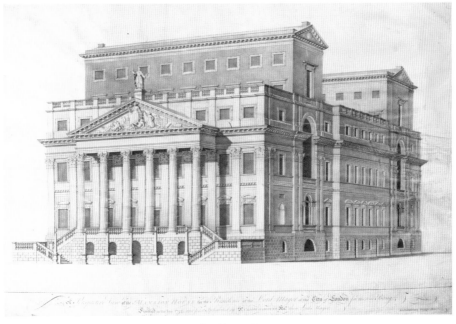

Perspective view of the Mansion House by Dance the Elder, 1753

Jones, Kent and Ware, and enlivened, when the house was nearing completion, by the latest Rococo ornament from skilled carvers and master plasterers.

Exterior

The north front of the Mansion House, facing the Bank road junction, has changed little since the eighteenth century. The six-columned portico survives, with a carved pediment by Robert Taylor showing the City of London wearing a turreted crown and supporting the City's coat of arms, trampling on Envy and receiving the benefits of Plenty brought to London by the River Thames. There were once high attics at front and back, known as Noah's Ark and the Mayor's Nest, which were removed in 1842 and 1795 respectively. The front steps began life as twin double flights flanking a small forecourt with obelisks and railings, but they have been reduced over the years as a result of road widening schemes.

Interior

Inside, the rooms in the Mansion House were originally arranged on four floors, with cellars below. The principal state rooms and accommodation for the Lord Mayor and Lady Mayoress were on the first and second floors, the ground floor was the domain of the servants and the

Above: Engraving of Robert Taylor's pediment design

Right: North-south section of the Mansion House as published in 1767

kitchen, and the third floor contained bedchambers. The first, second and third floors were built around a central courtyard or 'cortile'.

The first major changes occurred at the end of the eighteenth century, when George Dance the Younger, son of the original architect and Clerk of the City's Works like his father, roofed the courtyard, removed the Great Stair, and replaced the Egyptian Hall attic with a lower barrel vault. The house was then extensively refurnished and redecorated. James Bunning, Clerk of the City's Works and later City Architect and Surveyor, replaced the roof over the courtyard in 1861-2.

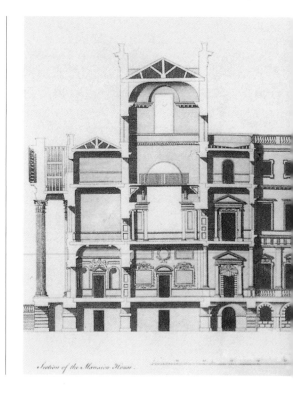

In 1930-31, under the direction of Sydney Perks, City Architect and Surveyor, and Sydney Tatchell, consultant architect, further major changes were made. Windows and a gallery were added in the Egyptian Hall, an additional storey was built to provide increased space for servants' bedrooms, and the whole house was redecorated.

The most recent work was carried out in 1991-3. This was a major refurbishment which included repair and conservation of the original fabric, installation of new services, reconstruction of some unsatisfactory later additions, replanning, redecoration and refurnishing. The work

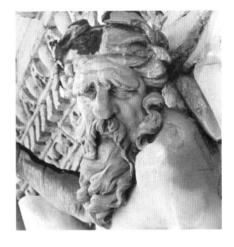

Detail of the river god on the pediment

was directed by the City of London's Department of Building and Services, with Donald W Insall & Associates as consultant architects for the historic areas and interior designers.

One of the principles of the interior decoration and furnishing scheme was that the house should be treated as a coherent whole. Very little of the original furniture survived, but several important suites of Regency furniture were reassembled, and a number of rooms appear as they might have done in Regency times. Decoration was in flat oil paint using colours mixed from eighteenth cent ary pigments. Historic fabrics and designs were selected for the carpets and curtains of the principal rooms, and a number of special light fittings were made. Existing furniture was restored and retained, with the addition of some special new pieces.

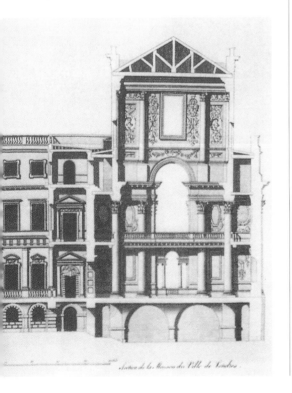

GROUND FLOOR

Entrance halls

The Walbrook Hall was originally intended to be a stable for eight horses, with a coach house to the south. The idea was abandoned once the house was occupied, no doubt for fear of the inconvenience and odour, but the floor was paved with stone and the space was used for storage. A coach house and stables belonging to the Grocers' Company were used, but eventually in 1770 new stables were built in Three

Walbrook Hall

Legged Court, Whitecross Street, to the designs of George Dance the Younger.

The main entrance to the house was through the portico on the principal floor, but the need for another more private entrance on the west side had been felt almost from the beginning. A west door had been made as early as

Waiting Hall

1757, but in 1846 it was decided that the redundant stable area should become a new entrance hall, with a large porch to give shelter from the weather. James Bunning was the designer of the new porch and the decorative plaster ceiling, both of which survive. The screen, derived from the Doric order of Bunning's porch, the wall brackets, the light fittings and the Purbeck stone floor all date from 1991-93.

This entrance hall is part of an extended reception area for guests arriving at the Mansion House – an arrangement which also dates from 1991-3. A new door in the east wall gives access to an Inner Hall, which in turn leads to the Waiting Hall. Both of these areas previously had suspended ceilings which concealed the original vaulting. Rustication was added to the piers in the Inner Hall in 1993. The ground floor halls are painted in a progression of cool and warm stone colours, with architectural details in white.

The carpets and rugs, woven by Woodward Grosvenor from an 1829 design in their archives, are deep red with oriental medallions. The curtains in the Walbrook Hall are of stamped moreen (a watered worsted cloth) woven by Context Weavers using the fleece of longwool sheep.

FURNITURE

The mahogany hall benches were supplied by John Phillips in 1811. They inspired the design of the new elbow chairs and side chairs, made by David Hordern in 1993. The eighteenth century hooded porter's chair used to stand in the first-floor vestibule.

SCULPTURE

WALBROOK HALL
The four plaster statuettes on the brackets are preliminary designs for four of the marble statues in the Egyptian Hall, submitted by the sculptors as part of their contract (see page 29).
South wall (left to right): *Penserosa*, Hancock; *Hermione*, Durham; *Timon of Athens*, Thrupp.
North wall *The Elder Brother of Comus*, Lough. Two more statuettes are shown in the North-West Staircase hall. The bust of *Queen Victoria* on the east is by Edward Onslow Ford (1898).

WAITING HALL
Six busts are displayed on scagliola pedestals made by Richard Feroze in 1993.
North side (left to right): *Russell Gurney, Recorder of London*, Hamilton Patrick MacCarthy (1879); *David Salomons, Lord Mayor 1855*, William Behnes (1858); *Major General Sir Henry Havelock*, William Behnes (1858).
South side (left to right): *Richard Clark, Chamberlain of London,* Robert William Sievier (1829); *Sir John Silvester, Recorder of London 1803-1822*, Robert William Sievier; *George Swan Nottage, Lord Mayor 1884*, Edward Onslow Ford (c1884).

PAINTINGS

WALBROOK HALL
North wall (left to right): *John Garratt, Lord Mayor 1824*, Thomas Stewardson (1825); *Harvey Christian Combe, Lord Mayor 1799*, Benjamin Burnell (1800).
South wall (left to right): *William Hunter, Lord Mayor 1851*, anon; *Thomas Quested Finnis, Lord Mayor 1856*, Thomas Roads (1850).

INNER HALL
View of the Mansion House, anon (c1760)

GROUND FLOOR CORRIDOR
South wall (left to right): *Gun Wharf, Tower of London,* Henry Pether (1863); *Custom House and Pool of London*, Henry Pether.
North wall (left to right): *The Thames at Westminster*, Francis Moltino; *The Thames near London Bridge*, Francis Moltino.

Gentlemen's cloakroom

Ground floor

Old Servants' Hall

This room has now been subdivided, and its principal features, the original chimneypiece and nineteenth century range, are part of the gentlemen's cloakroom.

Gold and Silver Vaults

The Gold and Silver Vaults contain a collection of pieces acquired for the Mansion House or presented as gifts to Lord Mayors and others. It includes the Fire Cup of 1662, which was saved from the flames at the Guildhall during the Great Fire of 1666 and is the only piece of City of London plate in its pre-Fire state, and the Lord Mayor's famous gold collar of SSs of c1520. He now wears a replica in gold of 1981.

The display areas in the corridors contain an exhibition of items connected with the history of the Mansion House which usually include some of the old copper cooking utensils saved when the kitchens were modernised.

North-West and North-East Staircases

The Mansion House had four staircases when it was first built – a Great Stair at the south-east which ran from the first floor to the second, a more modest stair at the south-west which ran from ground to second floor, and two staircases which

Gold vaults

North-West Staircase

ran from the ground to the third floor at the north-east and north-west. Of these, only the one on the north-east survives relatively unaltered. The Great Stair was removed in 1795, the South-West Stair was removed and rebuilt in 1931 and again in 1991-3, and the North-West Stair was modified in 1860 to make the treads shallower and the going easier, and was extended by a further flight to serve the new fourth floor in 1931.

Both staircases were stripped of paint this century, which is the way they would have appeared originally. They are constructed of oak – in other parts of the house the timber used was Norwegian yellow pine – and this finer quality wood was intended to be seen. The North-East Staircase has been left with the oak revealed, but because of the alterations in pine it was decided to paint the balustrade and the architectural details of the North-West Staircase again, leaving a polished oak handrail and treads. The festoon curtains here are of the same stamped moreen as those in the Walbrook Hall, and smaller elements of the carpet design there have been used for the bordered stair runners.

Lighting on the four principal landings is by lanterns in the Rococo style made by Wilkinson's in 1993, inspired by eighteenth-century examples and incorporating glass smoke dishes. In December 1987, Lord Samuel of Wych Cross bequeathed his important

collection of Dutch and Flemish seventeenth-century paintings to the City of London of London to be hung in the Mansion House. These are shown principally in the Saloon, the Long Parlour, the Drawing Rooms and on the North-West Staircase.

....

PAINTINGS

South wall of hall (left to right): *Winter Landscape with Duck Hunter*, Arent Arentsz; *Winter Landscape with Figures on a Bridge, a Hunter and Skaters*, Arent Arentsz.
Staircase wall (bottom to top): *Winter Landscape on the River Ijsel near Kampen*, Hendrick Avercamp (c1615); *Winter Landscape with a Frozen River and Figures*, Hendrick Avercamp (c1620); (above) *Panoramic Landscape with Shepherds*, Aelbert Cuyp (c1641-4); (below) *Winter Landscape with a Walled Castle*, Jan van Goyen (1626); (above) *Winter Landscape with Skaters*, Jan van Goyen (1646); (below) *Winter Landscape with Skaters*, Adriaen van de Velde; *Winter Landscape with Skaters*, Aert van der Neer (c1655-60).
Upper staircase wall
The Merry Lute Player, Frans Hals (c1624-8); *The Five Senses – Sight, Hearing, Smell, Taste, Feeling*, David Teniers the Younger (c1640).

NORTH-EAST STAIRCASE
Ground floor *Aldermen leaving Guildhall*, Ken Howard (November 1966).
First floor *Colonel Wilson, Lord Mayor 1838* and *Mrs Wilson*, attrib Charles Martin.

....

SCULPTURE

NORTH-WEST STAIRCASE
Plaster statuettes: *Caractacus,* Foley; *Sardanapalus,* Weekes.

First floor

Vestibule

Visitors arriving to see the Lord Mayor in the early years of the existence of the Mansion House came up the steps at the front of the house and entered by the main front door into the Vestibule. It was thus the first part of the house they saw, and was elaborately decorated. It has timber panelling – wainscot – on the walls, with an ornamented coved ceiling of plaster above. The stone floor is of Portland stone with black marble insets.

The specification for the plasterwork, signed by George Fewkes in 1749, described the 'moldings heads festoons and every other ornament' and the 'four Plaister Boys with two Shields containing the City's Arms'. Fewkes and his men also modelled the allegories of the four seasons after Boucher in the corners of the ceiling.

John Gilbert, who undertook most of the wood carving at the Mansion House, supplied the six Rococo brackets ornamented with delicately carved dragon-like birds amongst curling scrolls, foliage and flowers, which cost £210s each. They were made to carry candle lamps, and now support storm lights, made by Wilkinson's in 1993, with clear glass shades. The giltwood chandelier was made for the house in 1931 to the designs of Sydney Tatchell.

Vestibule

SCULPTURE

The six plaster statues were apparently among those loaned to fill the niches in the Egyptian Hall in the mid-nineteenth century. They are, from the front door, left to right: *Flora, Ceres, Abundance, The Fate of Genius, Rebecca at the Well*, and *Hermes*.

First floor

Private Secretary's Office and General Office

The two rooms leading off the Vestibule along the north front are used as offices for the Lord Mayor's staff. The north-west room contains the oldest grate in the Mansion House, thought to date from c1800, with an ornamental panel under glass showing a cupid riding a lion – an emblem of the taming power of love. It is set into the original marble chimneypiece of c1752, carved with the sword and scales of justice, because this room was intended to be the Cause Room or Justice Room where cases would be heard by the Lord Mayor as Chief Magistrate of the City of London. In fact, it has always been used either by the Lord Mayor or, more recently, by the Private Secretary. The giltwood chandelier dates from 1931. The festoon curtains are of green and gold striped moiré.

Bracket in the Vestibule supplied by the carver, John Gilbert

FURNITURE

The two mahogany bookcases with ebonised lions' heads were supplied in 1820 as part of the furniture of the breakfasting parlour or library. They complemented a set of six lyre back chairs, two of which survive, and the library steps which fold up into a stool, probably by John Phillips. The four new mahogany bergères by William Maclean, copied from originals formerly at Harewood House, recall those which were in this room in the Regency period.

PAINTINGS

South wall *The Card Players*, John Burnet.
West wall *Alderman Robert Waithman*, George Patten.
North wall *The Charlaton*, anon; *Grandpapa's Favourite*, Freidrich Meyerheim.

The north-east corner room on the opposite side of the house, and the larger room immediately behind it, were used together for justice business from the time the house was first occupied: the court was usually held in the larger room. The Justice Room moved out of the Mansion House in 1991. At the same time, the cells below, built in the nineteenth century and disused since 1982, were removed. The original marble chimneypiece in the corner room was taken out in 1810 and replaced by a much smaller one in stone. In 1991-3 the room was restored to its original shape by the removal of the partitions and the reinstatement of the west window. Before 1991, a door occupied the position of the window, which gave access from the portico to a corridor leading to the Justice Room. In these front rooms, the carpets and curtains in green and gold extend the colour scheme set by the carpet in the Venetian Parlour.

East wall *Portrait of a Lady* known as *The Countess of Ossery*, anon.
South wall *Miss Holcroft*, John Opie.

Esquires' Office

In the old Justice Room, now the Esquires' Office, the court fittings have been stripped out and the wall panels restored. What was the public gallery has been strengthened and refaced to incorporate a doorcase from the Egyptian Hall Gallery, made in 1931. The gallery houses the Lord Mayor's Diary Office, while the Lord Mayor's Esquires, the Swordbearer, the Common Cryer and the City Marshal, use the room below. The colour scheme of green and stone continues here. The room is lit by a large Venetian window with dark green wool damask reefed curtains, and carved and gilt wall lights by Edward Harpley (1993). The large central light inserted in 1962 remains.

PAINTINGS

South wall (left to right): *Sir William Treloar, Lord Mayor 1906*, Philip Cole (1907); *Sir George Carroll, Lord Mayor 1846*, George Holloway,
North wall (left to right): *Sir John Musgrove, Lord Mayor 1850*, John Knight (1852); *Sir Thomas Dakin, Lord Mayor 1870*, Henry Munns (1871).

The Lord Mayor's Office, known as the Venetian Parlour

Venetian Parlour

The Venetian Parlour, on the west side, was originally known as the Lord Mayor's Withdrawing Room and is still the room in which the Lord Mayor works and receives visitors.

The design of the plasterwork ceiling, executed by George Fewkes and his assistants, was inspired by a drawing by Giuseppe Artari, one of the most famous plasterworkers of his time. Over the Venetian window, which gives the room its name, appear cornucopias containing fruit and flowers on one side and coins on the other. The paint colours used, green walls and grey dado, were taken from the green, gold and white

Savonnerie-style carpet specially made for the room in 1976. A slightly bluer green was used on the walls for greater vibrancy. Most of the old gilding, which was in poor condition, was painted out. The reefed curtains are of gold wool damask, and the room is lit by the large giltwood chandelier of fifteen lights made for it in 1931 to the design of Sydney Tatchell, with new etched shades. The two smaller doorways on the north side are eighteenth century alterations to the original plan. The marble chimneypiece was supplied by Christopher Horsenaile in c1752 and is one of the most beautiful in the house.

....

FURNITURE

The mahogany desk ornamented with lions' heads, was part of a set of furniture supplied by Waring & Gillow in 1931 for this room. A pair of Regency style rosewood cabinets with wire grille doors are of 1993.

....

Saloon and Passage Room

This reception area was formed by roofing over the open courtyard or 'cortile', which was found to be impractical and damp. George Dance the Younger undertook the task of designing a roof, producing a number of different schemes. As built, in 1795, it was a simple structure with three circular lantern lights. This was replaced in 1861-2 under James Bunning's direction by a coved, partly glazed roof, which survived, with modifications, until 1991. It had been intended that this roof should remain, but prior to refurbishment the old roof was found to be unsound. A new roof was therefore designed with a simple steel and timber structure.

The space beneath was regularised by placing necessary services such as lifts and ducts in enclosures at the four corners of the Saloon area, rather than grouping them on two sides at one end as before. The new design brings daylight into the centre of the house once again with a large new octagonal lantern. The details of its Ionic entablature, in fibrous plaster, were taken from the antique Roman source of the Baths of Diocletian. Below is a plain coved ceiling, similar to many others in the house, supported on a Doric entablature, with details taken from Palladio.

Detail from a sketch by Dance the Younger showing an unexecuted proposal for the saloon roof, c.1793

Saloon

First floor

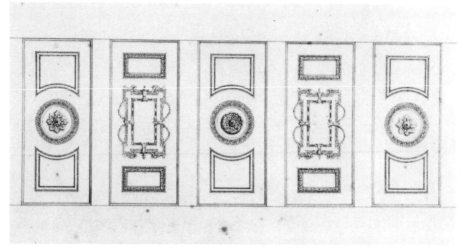

Design by Dance the Elder for the ceiling of the North and South Colonnades

Dance's original design was for a central stone-paved courtyard with low balustrading to east and west, and colonnades to north and south. The area leading from the Vestibule was known as the Passage Room and retains its stone paving.

The courtyard was, of course, open to the sky, but the colonnades had elaborate plaster ceilings, and six large plaster trophies on the walls, all of which survive. Although Dance made designs for some of these trophies when he first planned the house, they were not followed when the work was executed some years later. Instead, more up-to-date designs taken from engravings were used, whether at the suggestion of the plasterers or on Dance's advice we do not know. The trophies thus bring a distinctly French Rococo flavour to the ornament in this area. Their subjects include allegories of the Thames and the City (on the north), and Architecture and Fame (on the south).

The decoration of the Saloon is linked to the way the spaces were used originally. A rich ochre, the colour of Roman stucco, was used for areas within the building and a light grey for areas which were part of the courtyard. This suggests walking from covered colonnades to a lighter open space. The stronger ochre emphasises the trophies in the colonnades. The previously existing gilding was extended to the new features in 1993.

The Saloon is lit by a set of magnificent cut glass chandeliers, made by Messrs Osier in 1875, with a centre piece of 36 lights. The carpet, a crimson and gold cut-pile Wilton, was specially made for this area in 1972.

FURNITURE

The two gilt Gothic receiving thrones, covered in crimson velvet, were designed by John Gregory Crace for the reception of the Prince and Princess of Wales at the Guildhall on 8 June 1863, to celebrate the gift of the City's Freedom to the Prince, and were later presented to the Mansion House.

Six new mahogany side tables with black Belgian fossil marble tops were made by Restall Brown and Clennell in 1993. Their square, architectural shape derives from French Empire designs, and was intended to complement the chairs from the Nile Suite (see page 25).

PAINTINGS

The paintings from the Samuel Collection shown here are mainly domestic interiors, with landscapes in the Passage Room at the north end.

PASSAGE ROOM
West wall (left to right): *View of the River Lek*, Salomon van Ruysdael (1641); *Ships at Anchor in a Calm*, follower of Jan van de Cappelle.
East wall (left to right): *Evening Landscape*, Aert van der Neer (early 1660s); *A Ford*, Isack van Ostade (c1648-9).

SALOON
West wall (right to left): *Musical Company* (known as *The Young Suitor*). Jan Steen (1661 or 1664); *A Woman Selling Milk*, Nicolaes Maes; *Still Life with Fruits and Flowers*, Jan van Kessel; *Still Life with Beaker; Cheese, Butter and Biscuits*, Floris van Schooten; *The Oyster Meal*, Jacob Ochtervelt (c1664-5); *Portrait of a Man in his Study*; Gerard ter Borch (c1668-9)
East wall (right to left): *Still Life with a Pilgrim Flask*, Willem Kalf; *A Lady and Maid Choosing Fish*, Jacob Ochtervelt (c1671-3); *Breakfast Still Life with Roemer*; Pieter Claesz (1640); *Still Life with Jug*, Pieter Claesz (1644); *A Young Woman Sewing*, Nicolaes Maes (1655); *Interior with a Woman Knitting*, Pieter de Hooch.

SCULPTURE

Two full-length statues, originally Commissioned for the Egyptian Hall (see page 29):
Sardanapalus, Henry Weekes (1856);
Caractacus, John Foley (1856).
Four royal hosts in the window recesses:
East *Queen Victoria*, John Francis (1837); *The Prince Consort*, John Francis (1840).
West *Edward Prince of Wales*, Charles Hartwell (1921); *King Edward VII,* Albert Bruce Joy. Four new plaster busts inspired by eighteenth century casts after the antique (Cicero, Seneca, etc), acquired in 1993, stand on brackets in the colonnades.

36-light chandelier in the Saloon

Long Parlour

This room, originally called the Great Parlour, has always been used by the Lord Mayor for dining and receiving visitors, and is one of the most important rooms on the principal floor. Its walls are panelled, with elaborately carved friezes over the doors and it has a very heavily compartmented ceiling based on that of the Banqueting House, Whitehall, by Inigo Jones. A number of preparatory drawings exist for this ceiling, ranging from one by Giuseppe Artari with delicate swags of flowers, to a sketch similar to the executed design by George Dance himself. The windows on the Saloon side looked out onto the central courtyard when the house was first built, but were closed up when it was roofed in 1795, removing a major source of daylight. Nevertheless, the east side of the room retains the architectural details of its windows.

The original scheme of decoration and furnishing here, as for most of the house, was stone colour and white on the panelling and a white ceiling, with eight gilt girandoles holding three candles each against the wall piers and a glass chandelier for eight candles in the centre. There were crimson worsted damask festoon curtains, a large Turkey carpet, a large gilt leather screen at one end to keep out draughts, carved wood side tables with marble tops, and a set of mahogany folding dining tables and mahogany chairs which would have been

Long Parlour

set against the walls or out of sight when not in use. The room was provided with a built-in pot cupboard for chamber pots, as were most dining rooms of the time.

The present furnishings are designed to recall the original mid-eighteenth century character of the room as far as possible. The woodwork, originally painted because the Norwegian pine used was not considered fine enough to be left exposed, was stripped in 1962. In 1991 it was decided to repaint it, as originally intended, and the mid-olive-green colour was chosen as a foil to the paintings from the Samuel Collection displayed here. The deep red festoon

curtains are in a wool damask based on an eighteenth-century design known as the Banyan Damask, now in the Bath Costume Museum. The Turkey carpet is based on an old Yaprak design. The giltwood chandeliers were designed for the room in 1931 by Sydney Tatchell. Optical fibre lighting for the paintings is clustered around the top of each chandelier chain, allowing paintings to be individually lit with minimum risk of heat damage.

Of the two chimneypieces, the one on the south is original and of fine statuary marble, while the other one, in stone with marble columns, was added in the nineteenth century. The stone has been skilfully painted to imitate marble.

PAINTINGS

East wall (left to right): (above) *The Water Pump*, Adriaen van Ostade (later 1660s or 70s); (below) *The Sleeping Couple*, Jan Steen (c1658-60); (above) *Still Life with a Stoneware Jug*, Hubert van Ravesteyn; (below) *Portrait of a Young Man*, Gerard Dou; (above) *Still Life with Glass of Beer*, Jan Jansz van de Velde III (1649); (below), *Winter Landscape with Skaters*, Esaias van de Velde; (above) *Woman Making Lace with Two Children*, Pieter Cornelis van Slingelandt (1660s or 1670s); below *A Young Woman Stringing Pearls*, copy after Frans van Mieris.
South wall *Peasants Dancing in a Tavern (1675)*, Adriaen van Ostade (1675).
West wall (above) *Village Inn with Backgammon and Card Players*, Adriaen van Ostade (1674 or 1675); (below) *Tavern with Backgammon Players*, Adriaen van Ostade (1669 or 1674); (above) *River Landscape with a Village and a Landing*, Jan Brueghel the Elder (1612); (below) *Village Landscape with Figures Preparing to Depart*, Jan Brueghel the Elder (1613 or 1617); (above) *The Road to Market*, Jan Brueghel the Elder; (below) *Rest on the Way*, Jan Brueghel the Elder (c.1612); (above) *The Lute Player*, follower of Frans Hals; (below) *Young Woman at her Toilet*, copy after Gabriel Metsu.
North wall *An Eavesdropper with a Women Scolding*, Nicolaes Maes (1655).

FURNITURE

The side tables and chairs were supplied by Howard and Sons in 1931 in a style sympathetic to the original house. New tops to the tables, in Crema Valencia marble, were added in 1993. The set of mahogany folding tables, also of 1993 by Restall Brown and Clennell, was inspired by a drawing of 1752, but the detail of the carved cabriole legs was taken from the side tables. There are four drop-leaf tables and three leaves, which provide a flexible system to seat from six to 32 people.

First floor

State Drawing Rooms

This matching pair of rooms was created in the mid-nineteenth century. When the Mansion House was first built, the north room was known as the Common Parlour, and was used by the officers of the Lord Mayor's household as a dining parlour. Its decoration included four empty roundels over the doors, two on the north and two on the south. The east and west walls had three windows each, and carved frames with mirror glass on each pier. It continued thus until the mayoralty of John Wilkes (1774-5), when it became known as Wilkes's Parlour. He added new furniture, new light fittings and commissioned five paintings in grisaille for the overmantel and the four roundels.

The room to the south was occupied by the Great Stair, which rose from first to second floor. During the alterations of 1795, the stair was removed, and two new rooms were formed in its place, one above the other. At the same time, the windows giving onto the courtyard were blocked. No trace of them is now visible.

The new room on the principal floor was at first occupied by the officers of the household, but in 1822 it was decided that the upstairs drawing rooms were no longer convenient and that the two rooms on the first floor could be used instead. They were converted into a pair

South Drawing Room

A chair from the Nile Suite

by moving two of the roundels and two of the mirrors and frames into the new room, accompanied by copies of the plasterwork decoration and a replica of the ceiling. In addition, a new stone chimneypiece, marbled to imitate the one next door, was installed, and a painting was commissioned to adorn the overmantel. To furnish the room, the chairs and sofas of the Nile Suite were brought down from the drawing rooms upstairs. In 1835, the rooms were newly decorated, with striped crimson covers for the furniture and matching curtains.

Descriptions of the rooms in documents of 1835 and in the 1851 furniture inventory were the starting point for the redecoration and furnishing of the rooms in 1991-3. The self-striped crimson silk and cotton curtains, of a material known as tabaret, are lined with gold silk. The cornices have poles in grained rosewood with giltwood finials and rosettes. The chairs and sofas are also covered with crimson cabaret, with striped cotton case covers to protect them from damage. The Brussels-weave carpet with its looped pile is crimson with gold medallions, to a design of c1820.

The two chandeliers, of 20 lights each, were specially made in a tent and waterfall design based on an original of 1828 by John Blades. The green of the walls, a Georgian pea green much used in the late eighteenth and early nineteenth centuries, was chosen as a foil for the crimson furnishings, acting as a background for the paintings from the Samuel Collection and setting off the mahogany graining on the doors. Grained doors were first recorded at the Mansion House in 1761 and have been reintroduced in many of the principal rooms.

The ceiling and wall decorations were stripped of many layers of paint, redecorated and the detail gilded in 1991-3, and the chimneypiece in the south room was marbled again. The paintings from the Samuel Collection are hung as they might have been in the early nineteenth century, grouped closely together and several rows deep.

....

FURNITURE

The Nile Suite
A set of 24 chairs and three sofas was supplied in 1803 by John Phillips for the second floor drawing rooms at the Mansion House. They were grained to imitate rosewood with gilded details, and covered in yellow silk. These chairs and two of the sofas were moved downstairs in 1822, and were covered in striped crimson silk in 1835, with curtains to match. The two sofas disappeared from the records in the nineteenth century, but the third sofa remained upstairs and has now been moved to join the chairs. It provided evidence for the regraining and gilding of the chairs which was carried out in 1992-3. A new matching sofa was made to complete the suite.

The ornament on the chairs consists of an upturned anchor, a sword, and a coiled rope, in addition to lions' heads and paws. This, and their date, links them to the naval battles of Lord Nelson – especially the Battle of the Nile of 1 August 1798 – and explains why they have traditionally been known as the 'Nile Chairs', but the anchor and sword could also be read as referring to the Thames and the City of London

---

NORTH DRAWING ROOM

FIXED PAINTINGS
North wall (left to right): *Vulcan and Venus, The Toilet of Venus, Liberality and Morality*; all by Edward Edwards (1774-5).

PAINTINGS

South wall (left to right): (above) *Cavalry Battle on a Bridge*, Palamedes Palamedesz (c1630); (below) *A Young Boy Copying a Painting*, Wallerant Vaillant; (above) *The Smedestraat, Haarlem*, Gerrit Berckheyde; (centre) *Interior of an Imaginary Church*, Emanuel de Witte; (below) *A Fortified Moat or Canal*, Jan van der Heyden (c1670).
West wall (left to right): (above) *Landscape with a Grey Horse*, Philips Wouwermans (c1644-6); (below) *An Imaginary Town Gate*

with Triumphal Arch, Jan van der Heyden (1663); (above) *Landscape with the Kermis (The Rustic Wedding)*. Philips Wouwermans (mid to later 1650s); (below) *The Castle of Bentheim*, Jacob Isaacksz van Ruisdael (mid 1650s);(above) *River Landscape with Ferry Boat*, Salomon van Ruysdael (1650); (below) *Sailing Boats on a River*; Salomon van Ruysdael (1640s); (below) *Cattle by a River*, Aelbert Cuyp (c1650); (below) *Winter Landscape with Horse-drawn Sleigh*, Jan van Goyen (1645); (above) *Winter Landscape with Figures on a Frozen Canal*, Aert van der Neer (mid 1650s); (below) *Winter Landscape*, Jan van de Cappelle; (above) *A Hoeker Alongside a Kaag at Anchor*, Willem van de Velde the Younger (c1660); (below) *A Canal in Winter*, Aert van der Neer.

SOUTH DRAWING ROOM

FIXED PAINTINGS
South wall Two roundels: *Clytie and Cupid* (left) and *Neptune and Amphitrite* (right) both by Edwards (1774-5). Overmantel painting: *The Judgement of Paris*, William Daniell (1822-3).

Cavalry Battle on a Bridge, Palamedes Palamedesz

Two Smalschips off the End of a Pier, *Studio of Willem van de Velde the Younger*

PAINTINGS

West wall (left to right): (above) *Landscape with Cornfield*, Jacob Isaacksz van Ruisdael (1660s); (centre) *Panoramic View of Haarlem*, Jacob Isaacksz van Ruisdael (c1670); (below) *Wooded Landscape with Figures*, Jan van der Heyden (c1668-72); (above) *Wooded Landscape with the Ruins of a House*, Meindert Hobbema (c1663-4); (below) *An Estuary with Boats*, Jan van Goyen (after 1650); (above) *Panoramic Landscape*, Philips Koninck; (below) *Two Smalschips off the End of a Pier*, studio of Willem van de Velde the Younger (early eighteenth century); (below) *A Kaag Anchored by a Sandbank*, Willem van de Velde the Younger (1650s); (below) *A Weyschuit Coming Ashore near Den Helder*, Willem van de Velde the Younger (c1655); (above) *Hofstede Arnestein with Middleburg*, Jan van Goyen (1646); (below) *A Kaag and Smalschip near the Shore*, Willem van de Velde the Younger (c1660); (above) *Cottage on a Canal with a 'Trekschuit'*, Cornelis Vroom; (centre) *Cityscape with a Church and a Square*, Jan van der Heyden (late 1660s); (below) *Wassertor Kleves*, Jan van der Heyden (1660s).

North wall (left to right): (above) *View of the Boterbrug with the Tower of the Stadhuis, Delft*, Jan van der Heyden (mid to later 1650s); (below) *The Castle of Heemstede*, Gerrit Berckheyde (1662?); (above) *Brazilian Landscape with Native Figures*, Frans Post (1666); (below) *Brazilian Village with Buildings and Native Figures*, Frans Post (1643 or 1645).

First floor

Egyptian Hall

This, the largest and most important room, was built as a banqueting hall and is the culmination of the first floor state rooms, closing the vista from the main front door. It is still used for state banquets, dinners and receptions of all kinds.

Egyptian Halls were very fashionable in the eighteenth century. Dance the Elder probably drew his inspiration from the Assembly Rooms at York, where Lord Burlington had created his version of the Egyptian Hall illustrated by Palladio. The name derives from the fact that in his treatise Palladio had illustrated a hall based on the description of the Roman architect, Vitruvius, of which the main feature was a basilica-like structure with a high central section or clearstorey and tower aisles, and two orders of columns, one above the other. The style of architecture was, in fact, Roman, but Vitruvius believed that the Egyptians used such dining halls. When it was first built, the Egyptian Hall at the Mansion House had a high clearstorey with a flat ceiling, as shown by Palladio. This was removed in 1795 and replaced by the present coffered barrel vault to the design of George Dance the Younger. In c1845 the areas between the coffers of the vault were decorated with papier-mâché enrichments in the form of laurel-leaf hands.

Egyptian Hall

Further important changes occurred in the nineteenth century. Between 1853 and 1860, the City of London commissioned from eminent sculptors of the day seventeen larger-than-life-size marble statues for the empty niches, inspired by figures from English poetry and literature, thus acquiring a major collection of mid-nineteenth-century sculpture. In 1868 two stained-glass windows by Alexander Gibbs were installed, showing scenes connected with London's history. The Royal Window, at the west end, illustrates the signing of Magna Carta in 1215, and Queen Elizabeth's procession by water from the City to Westminster. The City Window shows Sir William Walworth, Lord Mayor, slaying the rebel Wat Tyler at Smithfield in 1381 and the procession of King Edward VI to his coronation. Decorative schemes in the later nineteenth century were very colourful, introducing stencilled patterns, marbling and wall paintings which survive.

Twentieth century changes have also affected the appearance of the hall. At the time of the lowering of the roof in 1795, the gallery which ran round all four sides was removed because it was structurally unsound, and was replaced by a small music gallery on the north. In 1930-31 a major programme of repair and restoration was undertaken, led by Sydney Perks. He was keenly interested in the history of the Mansion House and published a well-researched book on the

Preparatory design for the Royal Window at the west end of the Egyptian Hall,
and the window as executed in 1868, both by Alexander Gibbs

subject. With the consultant architect, Sydney Tatchell, he suggested the reinstatement of the gallery. It was built in 1930 together with the windows on the south side.

The decoration of 1993, in whites and greys, is close to the original 'stone-colour' and creates a noble appearance appropriate to this great classical eighteenth-century civic interior. The existing gilding was modified and reduced; gilded cornices and crimson silk velvet dress curtains with gold trimmings, taken from a design by Chippendale, were added at the Venetian windows, and the oak canopy which

used to stand behind the Chief Magistrate's chair in the court was adapted as a canopy of state, against which the sword and mace can be displayed when the lord Mayor is present.

The hall is lit partly by concealed cornice lighting, and partly by new decorative fittings by Wilkinson's suspended between the columns. These were based on early nineteenth century colza-oil lamps, with five burners in globes, cut glass dishes, and City shields and dragons on the reservoirs. The floor, which dates from 1957, is in Zimbabwe teak. The specially-woven carpet was adapted from a design of c1810 to incorporate the stylised flowers in the coffers of the ceiling.

A new fire-escape stair was built in 1991-3 leading from the south-east corner to an exit at ground level, which meant that the door in that corner was closed up and the original niche restored.

FURNITURE

A gilt chair of state, probably of c1825, is placed before the canopy and used by the Lord Mayor at dinners and banquets.

SCULPTURE

From left of the entrance, clockwise: *Alexander the Great*, James Westmacott (1860); *The Morning Star*, Edward Baily (1853); *Byron* after Baily; *Alfred the Great*, Edward Stephens (1860); *Timon of Athens*, Frederick Thrupp (1853); *Hermione*, Joseph Durham (1858); *The Elder Brother of Comus*, John Lough (1853); *Egeria*, John Foley (1853); *The Welsh Bard*, William Theed (1856); *Leah*, Patrick MacDowell (1853); *Griselda*, William Calder Marshall (1853); *The Faithful Shepherdess*, Susan Durant (1860); *Britomart*, Edward Wyon (1856); *Sir Walter Scott*, after Chantrey; *La Penserosa*, John Hancock (1860); *Alastor*, Joseph Durham (1860). Dates given are the dates of commissionary.

Alexander the Great *by Westmacott, and other statues in the niches of the Egyptian Hall*

SECOND FLOOR

When the house was first built, it was designed for entertainments on two floors, and the second floor rooms were included in the route taken by guests. They would be received on the first floor, and dinner would be served in the Egyptian Hall. On some occasions, ladies and gentlemen would dine together, but often the ladies went up to the second floor and observed the dinner from the gallery of the Egyptian Hall. Refreshments would be provided for them in the Ballroom or Dancing Gallery, and the Lady Mayoress would receive visitors in her own room on the east side of the second floor. Guests would circulate through the rooms, eating, drinking, playing cards, and listening to music. So the Great Stair, together with the other staircases, played its part in giving access to the second floor. Its removal in 1795, together with the removal of the gallery in the Egyptian Hall and the roofing of the open courtyard, signalled a change of fashion in entertaining, with guests using the first floor only, and soon afterwards the first-floor drawing rooms were created. This arrangement has altered little in the years since. The second floor now contains the private apartments of the Lord Mayor and Lady Mayoress.

North Gallery

This was designed to link the two sides of the house, and originally had a single doorway into the Ballroom to the north. In 1817 this central doorway was replaced by two smaller ones. The North Gallery now also provides access to the additional suite of service accommodation built in 1991-3 around the cortile for the Lord Mayor and Lady Mayoress, replacing earlier constructions. Paint was stripped from the panelling in 1931. The room was repainted in 1993, using the same colours as in the Ballroom. The festoon curtains and the seat covers of the chairs are of blue silk and cotton damask specially woven by the Gainsborough Silk Weaving Company to an eighteenth century design. The two chandeliers by Osler's were purchased in 1931.

PAINTINGS

Portrait of George Dance the Elder, Nathaniel Dance (c1765); *Portrait of George Dance the Younger*, Sir Thomas Lawrence.

FURNITURE

Two 'serpentine-fronted commodes' were supplied in 1752 by William Kilpin, William Chesson and Paul Saunders for the State Bedchamber for £45 the pair. They are the finest surviving pieces from original furniture of the Mansion House. The mahogany sideboard and two smaller side tables are of early nineteenth century date. The new set of side chairs, by the Classic Chair Company, based on an Irish Chippendale original of c1780, have frames of *Dalbergia odifera*, an exotic hardwood very close in density and colour to the Cuban mahogany used in the eighteenth century.

North Gallery

Second floor

Ballroom or Dancing Gallery

This room was one of the main entertainment spaces, and was lavishly decorated with carved panelling and ornamental plasterwork, much of which survives. The plaster trophies on the walls celebrate themes connected with music, dancing, drinking and love-making.

The original furnishing consisted of benches along the sides for the guests and a raised dais at one end for the Lord Mayor and Lady Mayoress, with brass chandeliers hanging from the gallery, and gilded girandoles holding candles on the walls below. The room extended upwards into a high attic, with windows along the sides and at the ends and a flat, decorated plaster ceiling. The attic was removed in 1842-3, and a new barrel vault was built to echo the one in the Egyptian Hall. When entertainments began to take place on the first floor only the ballroom fell into disuse: today it is rarely used.

The much-damaged nineteenth-century floor was replaced by deal boards in 1993, and covered with a blue carpet previously in the Egyptian Hall. The wall panelling is painted grey, the gallery railings blue, as they were in the eighteenth century and the walls above stone colour. The ceiling is in greys, with blue in the coffers and white enrichments. Twelve mahogany wall

Ballroom

lanterns of late eighteenth century pattern were installed in 1993. The sun curtains are of lined cream muslin from a pattern of c1812 at Castle Coole, Ireland, woven by Context Weavers.

FURNITURE

The four late nineteenth-century mahogany sofas are covered in stamped blue velvet. The sofas and chairs in the late eighteenth-century French style were acquired in 1896 for the drawing rooms.

PAINTINGS

North wall (left to right): *Sir Claudius Stephen Hunter, Lord Mayor 1811*, Samuel Drummond (1813); *Sir Matthew Wood, Lord Mayor 1815-17*, Thomas Phillips; *Henry Woodthorpe, Town Clerk, 1801-25* anon; *Sir Sills John Gibbons, Lord Mayor 1871*, John Williams (1872).
South wall (left to right): *Sir Christopher Clitherow, Lord Mayor 1635*, anon; *Sir Matthew Wood*, George Patten (1818); *Lady Knill*, E R Bennison (1895); *Sir Frederick Prat Alliston*, Charles Haigh Wood (c1908); *Lady Mary Clitherow*; anon.

North Bedrooms

The corner rooms on the north front of the second floor were designed as bedchambers and remain in use as such. They have been little altered, except for the addition, in 1915, of dummy doors and additional roundels and panels on the walls. They retain their marble chimneypieces of 1752 by William Barlow with carved overmantels. The central space – originally a withdrawing room serving the Dancing Gallery – was

Second floor

North State Bedroom

converted into bathrooms early this century, and a new escape stair was added in 1991-3 using the original stair, which ran from third floor to roof, as the first flight and copying its details for the others.

The State Bedroom on the west side has a French Brussels-weave carpet with a design of liles on a crimson ground, similar to a carpet in the Drawing Room at Belvoir Castle. Curtains, bed hangings and upholstery are of crimson silk damask.

....

FURNITURE

STATE BEDROOM

An important suite of rosewood and gilt furniture was supplied in 1802 for the Lord Mayor's use by John Phillips. The bed was described as Egyptian in Style, and the other pieces had large lions paw feet and reeded columns with stylised leaf capitals, perhaps intended to resemble palm trees and continue the Egyptian theme of the bed. The surviving pieces have been gathered together here. They include two wardrobes, two commodes, and a cheval glass. The five chairs with rosewood graining and cane seats and backs may also have been supplied by Phillips at this time. The bed which went with the suite was sold in 1824. Inspired by the descriptions of Phillips' Egyptian-styled bed, it was decided to construct a new domed state bed which was based largely on a design by Sheraton published in 1793. Its damask hangings are lined with gold silk, trimmed with crimson and gold fringing, cords and tassels, and crimson silk bows. At the corners are dragons supporting the City's arms and on top of the dome is a gilded Cap of Maintenance. It was made in 1993 by Edward Harpley with hangings by Cyril Littler.

EAST BEDROOM
The East Bedroom contains the French Empire style bed previously in the west room and a nineteenth century rosewood and gilt suite of furniture. Curtains and bed hangings are of dark green silk overprinted with a French design of 1802-5.

PAINTINGS

WEST STATE BEDROOM
An Austrian Prince, Alessandro Longhi; *Portrait of a Young Woman* known as *Flora Macdonald*, Allan Ramsay.

EAST BEDROOM
Antwerp Cathedral, David Roberts (1860); *The Church of St Stephen, Vienna*, David Roberts (1863).

Boudoir

This room was originally called 'The Lady Mayoress' Apartment' and was furnished as a withdrawing room. It was used as a bedroom in the early nineteenth century, and is now a private sitting room for the Lady Mayoress. It has been decorated in pale blue and white, and the furniture continues this theme. The curtains are oyster taffeta with blue and white cords and tassels. The floral carpet was woven to a design of 1805.

FURNITURE

The two serpentine-fronted mahogany chests were probably part of the original furniture at the Mansion House. The two gilt semi-circular side tables with inlaid tops are of c1800, and the satinwood veneered inlaid Carlton desk is of c1910. New furniture includes a set of five black lacquer and gilt caned chairs and a mahogany Regency style bergère. An antique George III sofa with black and gilt turned legs was acquired in 1993.

PAINTINGS

White Roses in a Glass Vase, Henri Fantin-Latour (1875); *Gladioli and Roses*, Henri Fantin-Latour (1880); *The Embrace*, Frederic Joseph Soulacroix.

Lady Mayoress' Boudoir

Second floor

Lady Mayoress' Bedroom

This room was created out of the upper part of the Great Stair, and has been in use as a bedroom ever since. It now houses part of the important satinwood suite supplied by John Phillips in 1804, and is decorated in a warm cream colour, with curtains and hangings of unglazed printed cotton from a Portuguese original, with flowers and exotic birds on a yellow ground, fringed in blue. The chandelier, by Osler & Faraday, was purchased in 1962 for the Long Parlour, and was moved here in 1993. The green carpet is woven to a design of c1840.

FURNITURE

Pieces from the Phillips' satinwood suite of 1804 include a serpentine chest, a fitted dressing table, a toilet mirror, and a cheval glass. A chaise-longue of c1825 is set at the foot of the bed. The satinwood firescreen with a cut glass panel is an antique piece acquired in 1993, as is the looking glass over the fireplace. The two oval satinwood

Private Drawing Room

Pembroke tables for the bedside, four satinwood elbow chairs with caned seats and painted decoration, the caned dressing-table stool and the carved and gilt wall mirror were all new in 1993. The large four-post bedstead finished in imitation of satinwood with painted decoration was specially made by Edward Harpley. The cornice is based on a Hepplewhite design published in 1787 (also used for the windows) and the posts are from a Sheraton design for a painted bedpillar published in 1793. Hand-painted prints from Bessler's *Hortus Eystettensis*, first published in 1613, hang on the walls.

Lord Mayor's Dressing Room

This 'South Gallery' was originally part of the grand route which led from the Great Stair to the Egyptian Hall gallery and other parts of the second floor. Since it was an important part of the circulation route during entertainments, it was elaborately ornamented with curving cornices and pairs of plaster cherubs. Now it is used by the Lord Mayor as his dressing room. The carpet is woven to a design used in Lord Byron's bedroom at Newstead Abbey of c1809. The decoration is in pale green with a warm stone colour and white, with Roman blinds in striped moire. The chandelier, by Osler, was previously in the Vestibule.

FURNITURE

The two wardrobes, the chest and the toilet mirror are from Phillips' satinwood suite of 1804. Later furniture includes two satinwood side tables and a washstand, and a set of five beech chairs with cane seats. Furniture made in 1993

includes a George III style satinwood library table and tub chair, a French cherry-wood bateau lit, veneered in satinwood, and a satinwood cheval glass copied from the Phillips' piece of 1804 by Restall Brown and Clennell.

Private Dining Room

Private Drawing Room and Private Dining Room

When the house was built, these rooms served as the Lord Mayor's Bedchamber and Antechamber. Later, they became drawing rooms, and the dividing wall was altered to make a large central opening. The windows looking onto the courtyard were closed up early in the nineteenth century because of the window tax, and replaced by niches. The rooms are decorated en suite in biscuit-yellow, with green and terracotta furnishings. The curtains are in a green silk/cotton damask woven to a famous eighteenth century design known as 'Bologna', 'Pavia' or 'Walpole' by the Gainsborough Silk Weaving Company. The chandeliers, by Osler & Faraday, were purchased in 1962 for the Long Parlour and were moved here in 1993. The carpet for the drawing room is from a design of c1814. In the dining room the carpet design was based on a painting of c1775.

The rooms on the third and fourth floors are used as family rooms or by the members of the household and staff.

FURNITURE

The most important pieces in the Private Dining Room are three mahogany cabinets, supplied by Robert Herring in 1825, ornamented with lions' heads painted to imitate bronze. 'The side table with lions' heads and paws was probably supplied by John Phillips early in the nineteenth century and the dining suite by Howard and Sons comprising a table, chairs, a sideboard and pedestals, side tables and a wine cooler dates from 1931. The furniture acquired in 1993 includes two Gainsborough chairs in old Cuban mahogany by Arthur Brett, reproduced from an original of c1740, and a red lacquer and gilt George I style pier glass by Restall Brown and Clennell.

PAINTINGS

PRIVATE DINING ROOM
Izaak Walton Fishing, Edward Ward (1850); *A Devonshire Stream*, Frederick Lee (1860); *Dutch Schuyts Beating out of the Scheldt*, Richard Beavis; *The Stream in Summertime*; Benjamin Leader (1863).

PRIVATE DRAWING ROOM
Skating, George Morland (1792); *The Wood Gatherers*, Jean-Baptiste-Camille Corot (after 1875).

FURTHER READING

Sally Jeffery *The Mansion House* Phillimore & Co, 1993

Lady Knill *The Mansion House* Stanley Paul & Co, 1937

Sydney Perks *The History of the Mansion House* Cambridge University Press, 1922

Dorothy Stroud *George Dance, Architect, 1741-1825* Faber & Faber, 1971

Original drawings for the Mansion House by George Dance father and son are in the collections of the City of London Records Office, Guildhall, and Sir John Soane's Museum, 13 Lincoln's Inn Fields, London WC2A 3BP.

Documents relating to the building of the Mansion House and its subsequent history are held at the City of London Records Office.

ILLUSTRATION ACKNOWLEDGEMENTS

Rob Brown
Pages 8, 9, 10, 11, 13, 14, 15, 19, 20, 23, 28, 31, 33, 34, 36, 37, 38, 39

The Guildhall Art Gallery, City of London/ Bridgeman Art Library

Pages 4, 126, 27

The Guildhall Library
Cover, pages 2, 6, 40

Sally Jeffery
Page 7

Museum of London
Page 1

The Royal Commission on the Historical Monuments of England, crown copyright
Pages 17, 24, 30 (right)

By courtesy of the Trustees of Sir John Soane's Museum
Pages 5,16,18

City of London Records Office
Page 30 (left)